THE UNITED STATES PRESIDENTS

DONALD
TRUMP
OUR 45TH PRESIDENT

by Ann Gaines Rodriguez

D1158217

The Child's World®
childsworld.com

1980 Lookout Drive • Mankato, MN 56003-1705
800-599-READ • www.childsworld.com

PHOTOS

Cover and page 3: Library of Congress, Prints and Photographs Division (detail)
Interior: Associated Press, 16, 17, 19, 21, 27, 34, 37; BRIAN SNYDER/ REUTERS/Newscom, 11; Dennis Caruso/NY Daily News Archive via Getty Images, 14, 38 (right); Donald J. Trump, Inc., 6; EVAN VUCCI/UPI/Newscom, 30; FloridaStock/Shutterstock.com, 15; GARY HERSHORN/REUTERS/Newscom, 20, 39 (left); Jeff J. Mitchell/Getty Images News via Getty Images, 26, 39 (bottom right); Jeffrey Asher/ Archive Photos via Getty Images, 4, 38 (left); JOHN ANGELILLO/UPI/ Newscom, 23; John Pedin/NY Daily News Archive via Getty Images, 12; Joseph Sohm Visions of America/Newscom, 24; JT Vintage/ZUMA Press/Newscom, 8; Judie Burstein/ZUMAPRESS/Newscom, 10; KEVIN LAMARQUE/REUTERS/Newscom, 29; Laura Cavanaugh UPI Photo Service/Newscom, 18; Lewis Tse Pui Lung/Shutterstock.com, 13; Nancy Kaszerman/ZUMA Press/Newscom, 22; Official White House Photo by Andrea Hanks, 28, 35, 39 (top right); Official White House Photo by D. Myles Cullen, 36; PAT BENIC/UPI/Newscom, 32; Richard Ellis/ZUMA Press/Newscom, 25; Seth Poppel/ZUMA Press/Newscom, 7; Shealah Craighead/ZUMA Press/Newscom, 33; Splash News/ Newscom, 5; Tom Allen/*The Washington Post* via Getty Images, 9

ISBN 9781503844360 (REINFORCED LIBRARY BINDING)
ISBN 9781503846890 (PORTABLE DOCUMENT FORMAT)
ISBN 9781503848085 (ONLINE MULTI-USER EBOOK)
LCCN 2020934903

Printed in the United States of America

CONTENTS

Donald Trump was sworn in as the 45th president of the United States on January 20, 2017.

CHAPTER ONE

A PRIVILEGED CHILDHOOD

Donald John Trump, the 45th president of the United States, was born on June 14, 1946, in Queens, New York. Queens is one of the five **boroughs** in New York City. Donald was the fourth of five children born to Fred and Mary Trump. Donald grew up with four siblings: Maryann, Fred Jr., Elizabeth, and Robert.

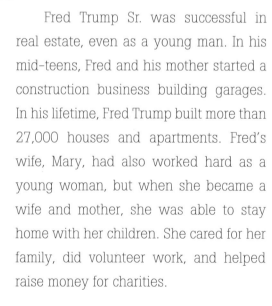

Fred Trump Sr. was successful in real estate, even as a young man. In his mid-teens, Fred and his mother started a construction business building garages. In his lifetime, Fred Trump built more than 27,000 houses and apartments. Fred's wife, Mary, had also worked hard as a young woman, but when she became a wife and mother, she was able to stay home with her children. She cared for her family, did volunteer work, and helped raise money for charities.

Businessman Donald Trump is pictured here in the late 1980s in Atlantic City, New Jersey.

Fred Trump was a prominent real-estate developer and became very wealthy. After his youngest child was born, he built his family a 23-room mansion (shown here) in the affluent community of Jamaica Estates in Queens, New York.

When Donald was born, his family lived in a small house. But when Donald was four years old, his baby brother Robert was born, and the family needed more space. Fred Trump built a much larger and elegant house. It had 23 rooms, including 9 bathrooms! Neighbors were impressed because the Trumps were now wealthy—they had limousines, a maid, a cook, and a chauffeur.

Although he was German, Fred Trump told people he was Swedish until the 1990s. He did so because of anti-German prejudice during World War II (1939–1945).

As a small boy, Donald attended a private school. His parents were strict. While Fred and Mary were wealthy, they encouraged their children to earn their own money. Donald started early, working as a paperboy and recycling bottles. At home with his parents, he was a well-behaved child. But when he got older, Donald sometimes got in trouble in school. Because Fred wanted Donald to learn discipline, he enrolled his son in a military academy. It was a boarding school, which meant that Donald lived in a dorm room and ate his meals in a group hall. At the New York Military Academy, Donald was very competitive. He played baseball and football. His senior year, he was a student leader. Donald was named captain of a corps of **cadets.**

Donald Trump graduated from the academy in 1964. After graduating, he thought about going to film school at the University of Southern California. But he decided instead to follow his father into the real-estate business. Donald enrolled at Fordham University in New York. He lived with his parents in Queens and **commuted** to school. He drove a red sports car that got him a lot of attention. While at Fordham, Donald played sports again, this time joining the squash team. Classmates remember that Donald also loved to golf.

Donald Trump attended the Kew-Forest School from kindergarten through seventh grade.

Donald (shown here during his senior year) graduated from the New York Military Academy in 1964.

A busy street view of Midtown Manhattan in the mid-1960s is pictured here. After graduating from Wharton in 1968, Donald began working full-time in the city, managing his father's many rental properties.

In the fall of 1966, Donald Trump transferred to the University of Pennsylvania, where he enrolled in the Wharton School. Donald stood out from other students there, because he often wore a suit and carried a briefcase to class.

Immigration records from 1885 list Friedrich Trump's last name as *Trumpf.*

When Donald graduated in 1968, the United States was involved in the Vietnam War. Men were being **drafted** into the military to fight in the war. As a student, Donald had received four **deferments.** This had allowed him to avoid being drafted while he was in school. After he graduated, a doctor diagnosed Donald with bad feet. Donald received another deferment, this time for health reasons. He never had to serve in the war.

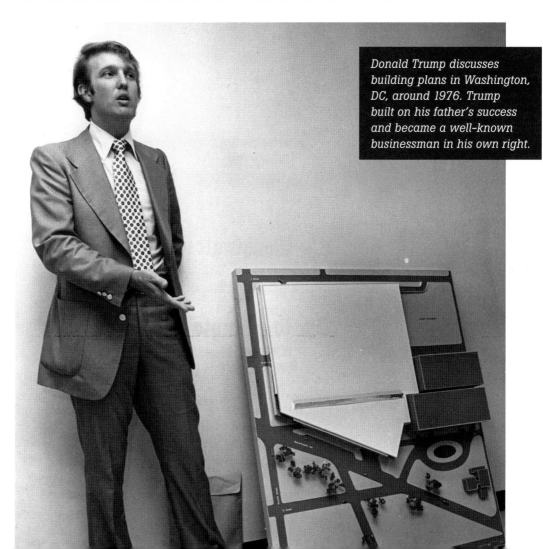

Donald Trump discusses building plans in Washington, DC, around 1976. Trump built on his father's success and became a well-known businessman in his own right.

THE TRUMP FAMILY

Donald Trump comes from humble beginnings. His grandfather, Malcolm MacLeod, was a fisherman in Scotland. The family lived on a farm, and they struggled financially. In February 1930, Donald's mother, Mary MacLeod, came by herself to the United States. At 18 years old, she came to work as a "domestic," or maid. In New York City, Mary lived with her sisters who had come to the United States a few years earlier. Her sisters helped her find work, and one night they took her to a party. There she met the man who would become Donald's father, Fred Trump. (In the photo above, Donald is pictured with his parents, Fred and Mary, in 1992.)

When Fred and Mary met, Fred was already making money. But his family had also been through hard times. Fred's father, Friedrich Trump, came to the United States from Germany in 1885.

Immigration records say Friedrich Trump was a farmer. Friedrich went to the Pacific Northwest, where he ran hotels for miners. After briefly returning to Germany, Friedrich and his new wife settled in New York. They started a family, and Friedrich again entered the hotel business and started to buy real estate. In 1918, Friedrich died in the influenza pandemic.

Fred Trump was just 12 years old when his father died. He quickly became head of the household, and eventually started his own construction company with his sister's help. By the time he met Mary, Fred was a successful businessman. Together they had five children, who spent time with their father while he worked.

In his own life, Donald Trump has been married three times. He has said that the first two times he married, he was not a very good husband. But Trump prides himself on the job he's done raising his children. He has five children, four of whom are adults. Like his father did with him, Donald Trump brought the children he had with his first wife, Ivana– Donald Jr., Ivanka, and Eric–to work with him. As adults, they have joined their father in his businesses. In their own right, they've been successful. In the below photo, Donald Trump's adult children, (from left to right) Donald Jr., Ivanka, Eric, and Tiffany, celebrate as their father was officially nominated as the Republican presidential candidate in July 2016.

CHAPTER TWO

DEVELOPING THE BRAND

After graduating from Wharton, Donald Trump went to work for his father. Fred Trump was building public housing in New York, including a giant apartment complex called Trump Village. In 1971, at the age of 25, Donald became president of his family's business, called the Trump Management Company. He handled the company's operations.

Eventually, Trump decided that what he really wanted to do was build. But instead of building more apartments, Trump wanted to build high-rises in Manhattan. In 1976, Trump started work on a very big deal. Together with the Hyatt Hotel chain, he bought the old Commodore Hotel and fixed it up. The old, forgotten building became a huge, modern, luxury hotel. Renamed the Grand Hyatt, the new hotel's rooms rented for as much as $1,100 a night. The Grand Hyatt project helped Donald Trump become well known in New York.

One of Trump's first major projects was buying the old Commodore building and turning it into a luxury hotel.

The Trump Tower is 664 feet (202 m) high and has 58 stories. The three highest floors make up the Trump family's residence, which is accessed from a private elevator. The Trump Organization's offices are also in Trump Tower.

TRUMP TOWER

Trump's next project was even bigger. In 1979, he bought property in one of the most expensive sections of the city. Construction on a huge building began, and in 1983, Trump Tower opened. The 664-foot (202-m) skyscraper loomed over Fifth Avenue. Fifty-eight floors high, it housed offices, stores, restaurants, and apartments. Visitors came just to see its lobby, which featured pink marble and gold-painted elevators. Donald Trump himself still has a luxury penthouse apartment in the building.

When Donald became president of Trump Management Company in 1971, his father served as chairman of the board. This meant Fred worked with investors.

Trump rebuilt the Commodore Hotel for $100 million.

When Trump purchased the property for Trump Tower, he also purchased the rights to the air space above the Tiffany & Co. jewelry store next door. That meant that another high-rise could not be built in that area.

Although Trump speaks proudly of his successes, there have been failures as well. Trump's businesses have had to file for bankruptcy six times.

In the years that followed, Trump bought a dozen more Manhattan buildings, including the famous Plaza Hotel. In 1986, New Yorkers raved when Trump paid for repairs to the Wollman ice-skating rink in Central Park. Over time, Trump began to acquire properties outside of New York as well. He opened casinos in Atlantic City, New Jersey. He bought country clubs all over the world, including in Scotland. One of Trump's most cherished purchases was the Mar-a-Lago property in Palm Beach, Florida. This resort and country club is one of his favorite places to rest, relax, and play golf. To this day, Trump spends as many weekends as he can there.

Trump and his father, Fred, attend the reopening of the Wollman Rink in Central Park. When the original repairs had stalled in the early 1980s, Trump took over the project and completed all the work ahead of schedule.

Mar-a-Lago was a 128-room mansion in Palm Beach, Florida, that was built in the 1920s. After he bought the property, Trump turned it into an exclusive resort.

In 1987, Trump cowrote a book titled *The Art of the Deal*. In it, Trump talked about growing up and starting his businesses. He also gave advice for business success. By 1988, Trump was reported to be a billionaire. The businessman from Queens was on the rise.

Mar-a-Lago means "sea-to-lake" in Spanish. It refers to the fact that the property extends from the Atlantic Ocean all the way to an area formerly called Lake Worth.

"THE DONALD"

From early on in his career, Donald Trump has enjoyed attention and fame. His first wife, Ivana, even gave him the nickname "The Donald," partly because of her husband's eye for the spotlight. By 1983, Trump was as much of a celebrity as some movie stars. Trump began showing up on talk shows, television episodes, and movies. He also began to branch out his businesses to include beauty pageants, a USFL team (the United States Football League, which played for three seasons from 1983 to 1985), an airline, a university, a magazine, and even steaks, bottled water, and a board game. The Donald seemed to be everywhere!

CHAPTER THREE

EMPIRE

As a businessman in New York City, Fred Trump got to know many city **politicians.** Donald Trump later said that his father had to do this, in order to get **zoning.** Donald followed suit, especially after he started to purchase and build on properties in Manhattan. Donald Trump had friends in both the Democratic and Republican **political parties**—it was part of being in business. Over the years, Trump gave money to candidates of both parties. He watched and learned how politicians worked.

Donald Trump poses outside the New York Stock Exchange in 1995.

Trump changed his political party views five times between 1987 and 2012. Trump first registered as a Republican, then as an independent, then as a Democrat, and then as an independent again. Finally, in 2012, Trump registered as a Republican once more.

In 2000, Trump considered a run for the presidency. He had already stated his political views publicly, in newspaper articles and in full-page advertisements. Trump decided to hire a **ghostwriter** to help him write *The America We Deserve*, a book in which Trump described his vision for the United States. Trump discussed **foreign policy** and economic ideas. At the time, he had some views he no longer agrees with. For example, Trump discussed raising taxes on the wealthy and banning assault weapons—two ideas he no longer supports. On the other hand, he also had views in the book that he continues to hold, such as supporting the development of charter schools and desiring a slowdown of immigration. Trump's book came at a time when it looked like there was room in the American political system for a third party. Trump wondered how he would do as a **reform** candidate. He decided the time was not right to run for president.

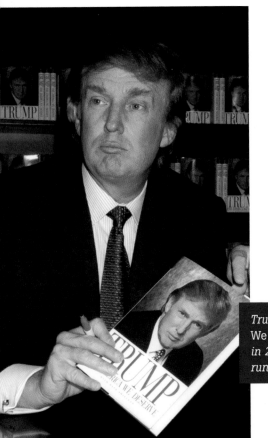

Trump signs copies of his book The America We Deserve *at Trump Tower in New York City in 2000. At the time, Trump was considering running for the presidency as a reform candidate.*

Trump is shown talking to reporters before interviewing potential contestants for his hit reality TV show, The Apprentice, *in 2004.*

This hardly meant, however, that Trump had decided to step out of the public eye. He was already famous on television because he owned beauty pageants, including Miss Universe, Miss USA, and Miss Teen USA. Then a television producer asked Trump to host a new reality TV series called *The Apprentice* in 2000. On the show, **contestants** competed for a chance to work with Trump's main company, The Trump Organization. Millions of viewers watched the show each week. Americans loved to repeat Trump's catchphrase that he told each week's contestant who was eliminated: "You're fired!" *The Apprentice* ran for four years.

Donald Trump and Melania Knauss attend a reception at the Museum of Modern Art in 2005. The couple married that year and had their son, Barron, in 2006.

Trump starred in a remake of his reality TV series, called *The Celebrity Apprentice*, from 2008 to 2015. Celebrities competed on the show to win a donation for charity.

Donald and Melania Trump's wedding was attended by many celebrities and politicians, including former president Bill Clinton and Hillary Clinton, who was a US Senator at the time.

In the meantime, Trump was continuing to deal in real estate, although his role was changing. Sometimes Trump had his name on buildings, even though he had nothing to do with their construction. Some of these projects were overseas. There were changes in his personal life, as well. Trump and Ivana had divorced in 1992. He had married actress Marla Maples in 1993. After Trump and Marla divorced in 1999, he married model Melania Knauss in 2005. Their son, Barron, was born in 2006. That same year, Trump built a golf course in Scotland, where his mother was born.

Some Americans thought Trump was doing things that demonstrated his likeability. To them, Trump was interested in the finer, more luxurious things in life, but he also seemed to be able to laugh at himself. As Trump's fame grew, however, a new side of the businessman began to show: Trump seemed willing to bully or humiliate people who angered him.

Trump thought about running for governor of New York State in both 2006 and 2014.

Trump received a star on the Hollywood Walk of Fame in Los Angeles in 2007. He is pictured here with his son, Barron, and Melania.

Donald Trump first used Twitter on May 4, 2009.

In 2009, Trump's fame moved to a new arena: social media. He enjoyed using the application Twitter, because he could communicate with thousands of people all at once. He could say whatever he wanted, and people could respond to him immediately. To this day, Trump continues to use Twitter—often several times a day.

On social media, Trump often spoke about political topics. He questioned everything, from economics to foreign policy. Trump enjoyed the way he could speak his opinions publicly and read people's reactions. Trump once again began to contemplate running for office.

On June 16, 2015, Donald Trump announced his run for the presidency in the 2016 election, saying, "The American Dream is dead—but if I win, I will bring it back bigger and better and stronger than ever before."

In 2015, Democratic president Barack Obama was nearing the end of his second term. Republicans were hoping to take back the White House in the 2016 election. Seventeen Republicans announced they were running for the office. Donald Trump decided the time was right. He made the announcement that he was running for president on June 16, 2015, in a press conference at Trump Tower. Trump felt the next president needed to address issues such as illegal immigration, American jobs, and the fight against **terrorism.** Trump posed in front of a giant red, white, and blue banner emblazoned with his campaign motto—Make America Great Again.

Donald Trump does not drink alcohol or smoke. He only sleeps about four hours every night.

People attend a campaign rally for Donald Trump on the USS Iowa in San Pedro, California. Trump discussed boosting support for the military and building a wall to prevent immigrants and criminals from entering the country illegally.

At first, Trump's candidacy was not taken seriously. After all, Trump was a TV celebrity who had never held an elected office. However, the fact that he was an "outsider" in politics made many people like him. Trump gained support among men and women who felt that the government was not helping them. They believed that Trump listened to their problems and had solutions. Thousands of people showed up at his campaign **rallies.**

While campaigning, Trump often talked about the changes he wanted to see in America. He didn't like immigrants who came here illegally. He said he wanted to build a wall to keep Americans safe and to prevent illegal immigrants and dangerous criminals from entering the country. Trump wanted to bring back American jobs that had been farmed out to other countries. He wanted **corrupt** politicians out of politics.

American presidential candidates are chosen through a **primary** process. In this process, members of the Democratic and Republican political parties vote for the candidate they feel they agree with the most. This process starts early in an election year. Donald Trump lost in the first primary, but he soon picked up more supporters. Trump began winning in more states. Trump was unpredictable, and some voters liked that. Trump did not like to read prepared speeches but rather preferred to say whatever came to his mind. Sometimes he was rude or politically incorrect. Sometimes he insulted other politicians. Many people did not agree with Trump's way of handling himself on the public stage. But other people did.

Trump often referred to the removal of corrupt politicians from office as "draining the swamp."

Presidential candidate Donald Trump speaks to supporters during a campaign rally in South Carolina in 2015. As his candidacy gained momentum, Trump drew larger and larger crowds at his rallies.

By spring 2016, Trump had enough **delegates** to win nomination at the Republican National **Convention.** He was officially nominated as the Republican candidate on July 21, 2016. That same month the Democrats nominated Hillary Clinton—former First Lady, senator, and secretary of state—as their nominee.

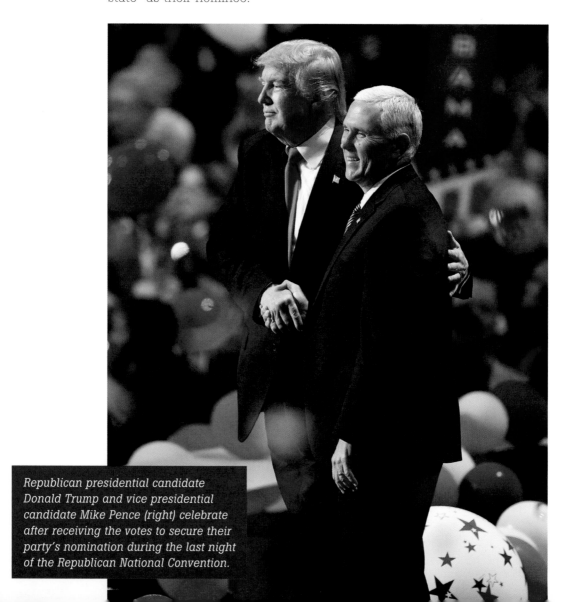

Republican presidential candidate Donald Trump and vice presidential candidate Mike Pence (right) celebrate after receiving the votes to secure their party's nomination during the last night of the Republican National Convention.

Donald Trump and Hillary Clinton engage in a heated debate for the final time in October 2016, just a few weeks before Election Day. The two candidates clashed over many issues, such as immigration, gun rights, and foreign policy matters.

In the months that followed, Trump and Clinton debated each other three times. Some of the debates got heated. The candidates each had their own ideas about how to best lead the United States. Heading into Election Day, **polls** predicted that Clinton would win the presidency. On November 8, 2016, Hillary Clinton did indeed receive more votes than Donald Trump. Almost three million more people voted for Clinton. However, American elections are not decided by popular vote, but rather they are determined by the Electoral College. There, Trump won in a stunning victory. Donald John Trump would become the 45th president of the United States.

The official voter count from the November 8, 2016, election was 65,853,516 for Hillary Clinton, and 62,984,825 for Donald Trump. That is a difference of 2,868,691 votes.

MELANIA KNAUSS TRUMP

Melania Knauss Trump is the First Lady of the United States. She is the second First Lady born outside of the United States (the first was John Quincy Adams's wife, Louisa, who was born in England). Melania Trump became a **naturalized** US citizen in 2006.

Melania was born in Slovenia, formerly Yugoslavia. She grew up in Sevnica, a small, picturesque town in the mountains. In high school, Melania studied in the capital city of Ljubljana, and she soon began working as a model.

In 1996, Melania moved to Manhattan to further her modeling career. She met Donald Trump at a party in 1998, and they began dating soon afterward. The couple married in Florida on January 22, 2005.

Melania Trump is a quiet, private person. As First Lady, she has an office in the White House. Children's issues are important to her, and in 2018 she began the Be Best campaign. It works to combat bullying and drug use. In the photo below, First Lady Melania Trump watches students conduct science experiments at an elementary school in Tulsa, Oklahoma, in 2019.

THE PRESIDENCY

Donald Trump had a lot to do before his **inauguration.** He had to settle many business projects and step back from leadership roles at his companies. This is because a president is not allowed to **profit** from his or her office. At that same time, he began to choose his staff and **cabinet** members.

On January 20, 2017, Donald and Melania Trump went to the White House to meet President Obama and First Lady Michelle Obama. Then it was on to the National Mall, where Donald Trump was sworn into office. He gave a speech in which he said the United States' situation was grim. He saw the nation as in great need of improvement. He said there had not been enough support of the military and that the United States gave too much aid to other countries. Trump said it was time to join "a great national effort to rebuild our country and restore its promise for all of our people." He said it was time for a new vision to rule our land. "From this day forward, it's going to be only America first."

The new president and First Lady smile at supporters as they walk in the inaugural parade in the nation's capital.

Trump's desire to unite the country was a daunting task. Instead of coming together, Americans became even more divided during Trump's first year in office. President Trump was slow to fill important offices and cabinet seats. The economy was strong, but Trump's policies were not creating the number of jobs he'd promised.

Perhaps the biggest problem for Trump arose over issues with the country of Russia. Even before Trump was inaugurated, there were questions as to whether Russians interfered in the 2016 presidential election process. A special lawyer and investigator, Robert Mueller, was appointed in 2017 to look into the matter. In 2019, Mueller released a report that said that Russia had indeed interfered.

Some people wondered if President Trump himself had cooperated with Russia in order to win the election. But Mueller's report did not find that to be true. Mueller's report, however, stated that there were areas where it appeared the president might have attempted to **impede** the investigation. It is against the law for any person to impede an investigation.

President Obama called Donald Trump in the middle of the night after his election win to congratulate him. He told Trump he wanted him to be successful. He promised that the transition to power would be peaceful.

The day after President Trump was inaugurated, a worldwide protest march occurred. More than three million women marched in the United States alone. Many marchers felt that President Trump had spoken rudely about women in the past. They also did not feel that he supported certain laws and rights for women.

The person who alerted officials to the phone call with President Zelensky was called a "whistleblower." A whistleblower is someone who exposes secret activities that are thought to be wrong or illegal.

In July 2019, a new problem arose. President Trump was on a phone call with the president of the country of Ukraine. Trump asked the president, Volodymyr Zelensky, to investigate a political **rival,** former vice president Joe Biden. Biden was expected to run against Trump in the 2020 election. Money the United States was sending to Ukraine for aid would be held up unless Zelensky agreed. A person listening in on the phone call alerted officials. It appeared that President Trump was asking for Ukraine's help in the 2020 election, which is against the law.

Donald Trump was sworn is as the 45th US president by Chief Justice John Roberts on January 20, 2017. Trump's family watched as he took the oath of office.

In June 2018, President Trump held a summit in Singapore with North Korean chairman Kim Jong Un. This was a historic event because it was the first time leaders from the United States and North Korea met in person. Some of the issues they discussed were developing peaceful relations between the two countries and denuclearizing (removing the nuclear weapons from) North Korea.

President Trump asserted that he'd done nothing wrong. Some people agreed. But the United States Congress had a job to do. They would have to investigate things further. They would need to interview witnesses to see if President Trump really was seeking foreign help to win in 2020. In September 2019, the Speaker of the House of Representatives, Nancy Pelosi, announced that a formal **impeachment** inquiry would begin.

House Speaker Nancy Pelosi (center) speaks to the press on Capitol Hill in Washington, DC, after the House of Representatives voted to impeach President Trump on two charges: abuse of power and obstructing Congress.

Andrew Johnson and Bill Clinton are the only other presidents to have been impeached. Johnson was impeached in 1868, and Clinton in 1998. Both were acquitted by the Senate and remained in office.

House representatives questioned witnesses and experts over the next few weeks. On December 18, 2019, the representatives had heard the evidence. With a vote of 230–197, the House voted to impeach the president on charges that he abused his power and that he **obstructed** Congress. President Donald Trump was now the third US president in history to be impeached.

Early in 2020, a trial in the Senate followed. The trial was required in order to determine whether Trump should be removed from his office as president. From January 16 through February 5, lawyers argued as to whether or not the president had really broken the law. In order for a president to be removed from office, two-thirds (67) of the senators would have to vote to **convict** him or her. On the charge that President Trump abused his power in the matter with Ukraine, only 48 senators voted to convict him. On the charge that Trump obstructed Congress, only 47 senators voted to convict. President Trump was not going to be removed from office. He was **acquitted,** and the trial was over.

On February 5, 2020, the US Senate voted not to convict the president. President Trump holds up a newspaper that announces his acquittal during a press conference in the White House the following day.

In 2020, a pandemic swept the globe, spreading a deadly disease called COVID-19 to every continent except Antarctica.

As his fourth year in office passed, Americans remained more divided than ever in their opinion of President Trump. His supporters liked that Trump was an outsider, and that he was unlike any other politician. They felt Trump was doing a great job. They pointed to the American economy, which had been healthy in the first three years of Trump's presidency. Trump's critics, however, maintained that he did not unite the American people as they felt a president should do—in fact, many felt that he created more division than ever before. In the future, Donald Trump's impeachment and personality may be what Americans remember about his years in office, but he himself believed that his presidency made the United States stronger and greater than ever before.

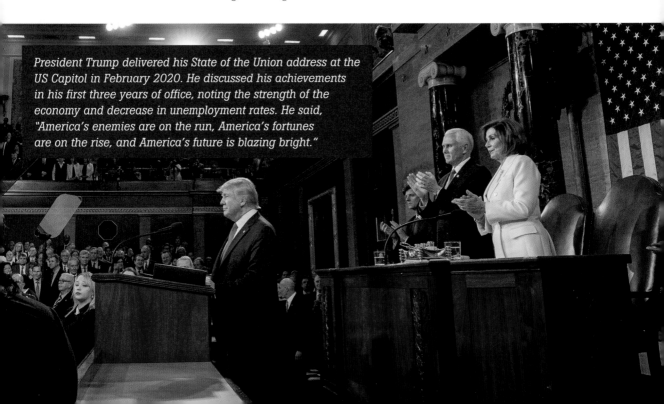

President Trump delivered his State of the Union address at the US Capitol in February 2020. He discussed his achievements in his first three years of office, noting the strength of the economy and decrease in unemployment rates. He said, "America's enemies are on the run, America's fortunes are on the rise, and America's future is blazing bright."

WHAT IS IMPEACHMENT?

When the United States was a new nation, the men who wrote the US Constitution understood that someday a president might be involved in a crime. Or perhaps a president might do something so wrong that he or she should no longer remain in office. The Constitution gives Congress the power to:

1. Impeach the president
2. Put him or her on trial
3. Convict him or her
4. Remove the president from office

This is how the impeachment process works:

1. According to the Constitution, if a majority of members of the House of Representatives vote that they believe the president has committed "treason, bribery, or other high crimes and misdemeanors," then they have impeached the president. Three presidents have been impeached: Andrew Johnson in 1868, Bill Clinton in 1998, and Donald Trump in 2019 (whose impeachment trial is pictured above). None was found guilty of a crime. In 1974, President Richard Nixon resigned before the House voted whether to impeach him.

2. Once the House has impeached the president, the Senate must put him or her on trial. During the trial, the Senate hears evidence of the president's wrongdoing. The president's lawyers defend his or her actions. Then the senators vote. If two-thirds or more of the senators vote to convict, then the president must be removed from office. If less than two-thirds of the senators vote to convict, the president is acquitted and remains in office. (The Constitution allows Congress to impeach the vice president and other civil officers of the United States. Civil officers include judges and other important government officials.)

TIME LINE

1940–1960

1946
Donald Trump is born on June 14 in Queens, New York.

1959
Donald is sent to boarding school at the New York Military Academy.

1966
Donald transfers from Fordham University in New York to the Wharton School of the University of Pennsylvania.

1970

1971
Donald moves to Manhattan, New York. He becomes president of the Trump Management Company, his family's business.

1977
Trump marries Ivana Zelníčková. Their first child, Donald Jr., is born in December.

1980

1981
Ivanka Trump is born.

1982
The Trump Tower is finished.

1984
Eric Trump is born.

1987
The Art of the Deal is published.

1989
Donald Trump appears on cover of *Time* magazine for the first time. Trump's Taj Mahal casino opens in Atlantic City, New Jersey.

1990

1991
Trump is forced to file for bankruptcy for the first time.

1992
Donald and Ivana Trump divorce.

1993
Trump marries Marla Maples. Their daughter, Tiffany, is born.

1996
Trump acquires beauty pageants, including Miss Universe.

1999
Trump and Maples divorce.

2000   2010   2020

2000
The America We Deserve is published.

2004
The Apprentice debuts on TV.

2005
Trump marries Melania Knauss.

2006
Melania Trump becomes a US citizen. Their son, Barron Trump, is born.

2008
The Celebrity Apprentice debuts on TV.

2015
Trump makes a bid for the presidency.

2016
Donald Trump is elected president by the Electoral College, defeating Hillary Clinton.

2017
Trump is inaugurated on January 20.

2018
In June, Trump holds a historic summit with North Korean dictator Kim Jong Un; in July, he has a meeting with Russian president Vladimir Putin; in December, the US government is forced to shut down for a record 35 days.

2019
The Mueller Report is released in March; in July, Donald Trump makes a questionable phone call to the president of Ukraine, causing a whistleblower to alert officials. On September 24, House Speaker Nancy Pelosi announces a formal impeachment inquiry will begin. The House votes to impeach President Trump on December 18.

2020
President Trump's impeachment trial begins on January 16. The Senate votes to acquit him on February 5.

acquitted (uh-KWIH-ted): Acquitted means found not guilty of a crime. Donald Trump was acquitted during his impeachment trial.

bankruptcy (BANK-rupt-see): Bankruptcy is when an individual or a business is facing financial failure and can't pay debts. Over the years, Trump's businesses have had to file for bankruptcy.

boroughs (BUR-ohs): A borough is a section of a large city that has its own government. Donald Trump grew up in Queens, which is one of five boroughs in New York City.

cabinet (KAB-nit): A cabinet is the group of people who advise a president. Leading up to his inauguration, Trump began choosing members of his cabinet.

cadets (kuh-DETS): Cadets are officers in training or students attending a military school. Trump was a cadet while he attended the New York Military Academy.

candidate (KAN-duh-dayt): A candidate is someone running in an election. Donald Trump was the Republican candidate in the 2016 presidential election.

commuted (kuh-MYOO-ted): To commute means to travel back and forth regularly. While Trump attended college, he lived with his parents and commuted to campus.

contestants (kun-TES-tunts): Contestants are people who compete against one another in a contest. Contestants in *The Apprentice* competed against each other to win a chance to work at the Trump Organization.

convention (kun-VEN-shun): A convention is a meeting. The political parties each hold a national convention every four years to choose a presidential candidate.

convict (kuhn-VIKT): To convict someone means finding or proving that the person is guilty of a crime. When President Trump was impeached, the Senate did not have enough votes to convict him of the charges.

corrupt (ku-RUPT): If people are corrupt, they act improperly for their own benefit, such as by taking bribes. In his campaign speeches, Trump promised to remove corrupt politicians if he was elected president.

deferments (di-FUR-munts): A deferment is the act of delaying or postponing something. When Trump was in college, he received deferments that allowed him to avoid serving in the military during the Vietnam War.

delegates (DEL-uh-gayts): Delegates are representatives who are chosen or elected to vote or act for others. At the Republican National Convention, Trump had enough delegates to win the nomination as the Republican presidential candidate in the 2016 election.

drafted (DRAF-ted): When people are drafted, they are required by law to join the military. During the Vietnam War, thousands of young American men were drafted into the military.

foreign policy (FOR-un PAWL-uh-see): A foreign policy is the strategies and plans a country holds to achieve its own goals or to protect its national interests in dealing with other nations. Trump shared his thoughts on US foreign policy in his 2000 book, *The America We Deserve*.

ghostwriter (GOHST-ry-tur): A ghostwriter is someone who is hired to write something (such as a speech or a book) for another person. Trump worked with a ghostwriter on his book *The America We Deserve*.

impeachment (im-PEECH-ment): Impeachment is when the House of Representatives votes to charge a president or vice president with a crime or serious misdeed. Trump was the third president to have impeachment proceedings brought against him.

impede (im-PEED): To impede is to slow the progress of or interfere with something or someone. In his findings, investigator Robert Mueller wrote that President Trump may have attempted to impede the Russia investigation.

inauguration (ih-nawg-yuh-RAY-shun): An inauguration is the ceremony that takes place when a new president begins a term. Trump's inauguration took place on January 20, 2017.

naturalized (NA-chu-ru-lized): Naturalized is when someone who was born in a different country is allowed to become a new citizen. Melania Trump became a naturalized US citizen in 2006.

obstructed (ob-STRUK-ted): To obstruct is to slow or block the moment or progress of something. In 2019, the House of Representatives voted to impeach the president on charges that he abused his power and obstructed the investigation.

pandemic (pan-DEM-ik): A pandemic is something (like a disease) that occurs over a wide geographic area and affects a high proportion of the population. Donald Trump's grandfather, Friedrich Trump, died in the influenza pandemic in 1918.

political parties (puh-LIT-uh-kul PAR-teez): Political parties are groups of people who share similar ideas about how to run a government. The two major political parties in the United States are the Democratic Party and the Republican Party.

politicians (pawl-uh-TISH-unz): Politicians are men and women who hold an office in government. Donald Trump and his father, Fred, worked with many politicians on their building and real-estate projects over the years.

polls (POHLZ): Polls are surveys of people's opinions on subjects. On Election Day of November 2016, most polls predicted that Hillary Clinton would win the presidency.

prejudice (PREJ-uh-dis): Prejudice is having a bad opinion about someone without good reason. Fred Trump didn't tell others of his German ancestry because of prejudice against Germans during World War II.

primary (PRY-mayr-ee): A primary is an election in which people of the same political party run against each other for the chance to become their party's candidate. Donald Trump won the primary election and became the Republican presidential candidate.

profit (PRAH-fit): A profit is money that is left over after all of the expenses of running a business are subtracted from the total amount of money earned. When Trump was elected president, he had to separate himself from his businesses because a president cannot profit from his or her office.

rallies (RAL-eez): A rally is a public gathering or meeting to support or oppose someone or something. Thousands of people attended Trump's campaign rallies.

reform (rih-FORM): To reform something is to improve it or correct the faults in it. The Reform Party in the United States is a political party that serves as an alternate to the Republican and Democratic parties. Trump considered running as a reform candidate in the 2000 presidential election.

registered (RE-juh-sturd): When you register for or as something, you enter your name on an official list that indicates which group you belong to. Donald Trump registered as a member of the Republican Party in 2012.

resigned (ree-ZINED): A person who resigned from a job gave it up. President Richard Nixon resigned from office before the House of Representatives voted whether to impeach him.

rival (RY-vul): A rival is a competitor. Joe Biden and Donald Trump are political rivals.

terrorism (TER-ur-ih-zum): Terrorism is the use of fear and violence to achieve a goal (such as the September 11 terrorist attacks in the United States). When Trump announced that he was running for the presidency, the fight against terrorism was one of his main issues.

zoning (ZOHN-ing): Zoning refers to a system of rules used to determine where homes and businesses are built in a city or town. Donald Trump and his father, Fred, became friendly with city politicians to help them get zoning approved for their many properties.

THE UNITED STATES GOVERNMENT

The United States government is divided into three equal branches: the executive, the legislative, and the judicial. This division helps prevent abuses of power because each branch has to answer to the other two. No one branch can become too powerful.

EXECUTIVE BRANCH

President
Vice President
Departments

The job of the executive branch is to enforce the laws. It is headed by the president, who serves as the spokesperson for the United States around the world. The president has the power to sign bills into law. He or she also appoints important officials, such as federal judges, who are then confirmed by the US Senate. The president is also the commander in chief of the US military. He or she is assisted by the vice president, who takes over if the president dies or cannot carry out the duties of the office.

The executive branch also includes various departments, each focused on a specific topic. They include the Defense Department, the Justice Department, and the Agriculture Department. The department heads, along with other officials such as the vice president, serve as the president's closest advisers, called the cabinet.

LEGISLATIVE BRANCH

Congress: Senate and the
House of Representatives

The job of the legislative branch is to make the laws. It consists of Congress, which is divided into two parts: the Senate and the House of Representatives. The Senate has 100 members, and the House of Representatives has 435 members. Each state has two senators. The number of representatives a state has varies depending on the state's population.

Besides making laws, Congress also passes budgets and enacts taxes. In addition, it is responsible for declaring war, maintaining the military, and regulating trade with other countries.

JUDICIAL BRANCH

Supreme Court
Courts of Appeals
District Courts

The job of the judicial branch is to interpret the laws. It consists of the nation's federal courts. Trials are held in district courts. During trials, judges must decide what laws mean and how they apply. Courts of appeals review the decisions made in district courts.

The nation's highest court is the Supreme Court. If someone disagrees with a court of appeals ruling, he or she can ask the Supreme Court to review it. The Supreme Court may refuse. The Supreme Court makes sure that decisions and laws do not violate the Constitution.

CHOOSING THE PRESIDENT

It may seem odd, but American voters don't elect the president directly. Instead, the president is chosen using what is called the Electoral College.

Each state gets as many votes in the Electoral College as its combined total of senators and representatives in Congress. For example, Iowa has two senators and four representatives, so it gets six electoral votes. Although the District of Columbia does not have any voting members in Congress, it gets three electoral votes. Usually, the candidate who wins the most votes in any given state receives all of that state's electoral votes.

To become president, a candidate must get more than half of the Electoral College votes. There are a total of 538 votes in the Electoral College, so a candidate needs 270 votes to win. If nobody receives 270 Electoral College votes, the House of Representatives chooses the president.

With the Electoral College system, the person who receives the most votes nationwide does not always receive the most electoral votes. This happened most recently in 2016, when Hillary Clinton received nearly 2.9 million more national votes than Donald J. Trump. Trump became president because he had more Electoral College votes.

The White House is the official home of the president of the United States. It is located at 1600 Pennsylvania Avenue NW in Washington, DC. In 1792, a contest was held to select the architect who would design the president's home. James Hoban won. Construction took eight years.

The first president, George Washington, never lived in the White House. The second president, John Adams, moved into the house in 1800, though the inside was not yet complete. During the War of 1812, British soldiers burned down much of the White House. It was rebuilt several years later.

The White House was changed through the years. Porches were added, and President Theodore Roosevelt added the West Wing. President William Taft changed the shape of the presidential office, making it into the famous Oval Office. While Harry Truman was president, the old house was discovered to be structurally weak. All the walls were reinforced with steel, and the rooms were rebuilt.

Today, the White House has 132 rooms (including 35 bathrooms), 28 fireplaces, and 3 elevators. It takes 570 gallons of paint to cover the outside of the six-story building. The White House provides the president with many ways to relax. It includes a putting green, a jogging track, a swimming pool, a basketball and tennis court, and beautifully landscaped gardens. The White House also has a movie theater, a billiard room, and a one-lane bowling alley.

PRESIDENTIAL PERKS

The job of president of the United States is challenging. It is probably one of the most stressful jobs in the world. Because of this, presidents are paid well, though not nearly as well as the leaders of large corporations. In 2020, the president earned $400,000 a year. Presidents also receive extra benefits that make the demanding job a little more appealing.

★ **Camp David:** In the 1940s, President Franklin D. Roosevelt chose this heavily wooded spot in the mountains of Maryland to be the presidential retreat, where presidents can relax. Even though it is a retreat, world business is conducted there. Most famously, President Jimmy Carter met with Middle Eastern leaders at Camp David in 1978. The result was a peace agreement between Israel and Egypt.

★ *Air Force One:* The president flies on a jet called *Air Force One*. It is a Boeing 747-200B that has been modified to meet the president's needs. *Air Force One* is the size of a large home. It is equipped with a dining room, sleeping quarters, a conference room, and office space. It also has two kitchens that can provide food for up to 100 people.

★ **The Secret Service:** While not the most glamorous of the president's perks, the Secret Service is one of the most important. The Secret Service is a group of highly trained agents who protect the president and the president's family.

★ **The Presidential State Car:** The presidential state car is a customized Cadillac limousine. It has been armored to protect the president in case of attack. Inside the plush car are a foldaway desk, an entertainment center, and a communications console.

★ **The Food:** The White House has five chefs who will make any food the president wants. The White House also has an extensive wine collection and vegetable and fruit gardens.

★ **Retirement:** A former president receives a pension, or retirement pay, of just under $208,000 a year. Former presidents also receive health care coverage and Secret Service protection for the rest of their lives.

FACTS

QUALIFICATIONS

To run for president, a candidate must
- ★ be at least 35 years old
- ★ be a citizen who was born in the United States
- ★ have lived in the United States for 14 years

TERM OF OFFICE

A president's term of office is four years. No president can stay in office for more than two terms.

ELECTION DATE

The presidential election takes place every four years on the first Tuesday after November 1.

INAUGURATION DATE

Presidents are inaugurated on January 20.

OATH OF OFFICE

I do solemnly swear I will faithfully execute the office of the President of the United States and will to the best of my ability preserve, protect, and defend the Constitution of the United States.

WRITE A LETTER TO THE PRESIDENT

One of the best things about being a US citizen is that Americans get to participate in their government. They can speak out if they feel government leaders aren't doing their jobs. They can also praise leaders who are going the extra mile. Do you have something you'd like the president to do? Should the president worry more about the environment and the effects of climate change? Should the government spend more money on our schools? You can write a letter to the president to say how you feel!

> 1600 Pennsylvania Avenue NW
> Washington, DC 20500

You can even write a message to the president at **whitehouse.gov/contact**.

FOR MORE INFORMATION

BOOKS

Houser, Grace. *Understanding US Elections and the Electoral College*. New York, NY: PowerKids, 2018.

Nagelhout, Ryan. *Before Donald Trump Was President*. New York, NY: Gareth Stevens, 2018.

Oachs, Emily Rose. *Melania Trump: Champion for Youth*. Mankato, MN: The Child's World, 2018.

Rubinstein, Justine. *Impeachment*. Philadelphia, PA: Mason Crest, 2019.

Sherman, Jill. *Donald Trump: Outspoken Personality and President*. Minneapolis, MN: Lerner, 2017.

INTERNET SITES

Visit our website for lots of links about
Donald Trump and other US presidents:

childsworld.com/links

Note to Parents, Teachers, and Librarians: We routinely verify our web links to make sure they are safe, active sites. Encourage your readers to check them out!